Take Charge

The proven action plan to secure your future through real estate transactions

Anthony Joseph

Take Charge

First published in 2021

Print: 978-1-922456-86-1
E-book: 978-1-922456-87-8
Hardback: 978-1-922456-85-4

Because of the dynamic nature of the Internet, any web addresses or links contained in this book may have changed since publication and may no longer be valid. The information in this book is based on the author's experiences and opinions. The views expressed in this book are solely those of the author and do not necessarily reflect the views of the publisher; the publisher hereby disclaims any responsibility for them.

The author of this book does not dispense any form of medical, legal, financial, or technical advice either directly or indirectly. The intent of the author is solely to provide information of a general nature to help you in your quest for personal development and growth. In the event you use any of the information in this book, the author and the publisher assume no responsibility for your actions. If any form of expert assistance is required, the services of a competent professional should be sought.

Publishing information
Publishing, design, and production facilitated by Passionpreneur Publishing,
A division of Passionpreneur Organization Pty Ltd, ABN: 48640637529

www.PassionpreneurPublishing.com
Melbourne, VIC | Australia

TABLE OF CONTENTS

To my family and friends, and everyone who inspired me in their own way, even if they don't know about it.

ACKNOWLEDGEMENTS

I'd like to acknowledge Moustafa Hamwi and his team at Passionpreneur Publishing for guiding me through the journey of making this book a reality.

Introduction

It took me thirty years to find my purpose in life. Before that, my life was filled with sadness, anger, and loneliness due to a lack of clarity about what I wanted to do with my life.

All that changed when I took charge of my life and BOSSED UP. Things started getting better, and I found a place for myself in this world—a place that I had yearned for and that now makes me extremely proud. I know there are thousands maybe even millions of people out there in the world who dream of achieving big in their lives but don't know where to start or how to go about it. That is why I wrote this book—so I can pass on my message and the lessons I have learnt to all my readers.

I come from a broken family; my parents divorced when I was just eight years old. I lived all my teenage days recklessly, with no goals and no hope, just surviving day-by-day and wondering what my purpose was in life. But when I decided I wanted to turn my life around with all my heart and mind, that's when things started to change. And believe me, I am living proof that anyone can make it if they show enough perseverance, determination, and willpower.

If you are someone who dreams of making it big like me, go ahead and turn the page. This book will teach you what they don't teach you in schools or universities: it will teach you how to change your mindset and become the best version of yourself, just like I did.

CHAPTER 1

HOW IT ALL STARTED

Things don't get easy; you get stronger.

Nothing can stop you from achieving your dreams if you have the drive to do so and keep persevering to reach them.

I still remember the day I moved to Dubai from my home country, Lebanon. It was the 23rd of October in the year 2014. I was sad and heartbroken to have left behind everything I knew and loved—my family, friends, and the place I grew up in. All I had with me was $1000 and this feeling of insecurity about how I was going to make it in a city that was new to me.

I was received by my uncle, whom I last saw when I was three years old; however, seeing a familiar face in a strange land instilled a sense of comfort in me. Slowly, I started getting excited about my new life in Dubai, which everyone spoke about as the city where dreams come true.

As we drove out of the airport to where my uncle lived, I saw humongous high-rises towering over the roads. It was surreal. When my uncle asked me how I felt, I could say nothing; all I could do was experience these mixed emotions—the joy of being in a new city, the excitement of experiencing such beauty for the first time, sadness due to leaving my old life behind, and tiredness because of the journey I had just had.

It was the first time I had left my comfort zone behind—and only on a hunch that I would have a better, more fulfilling life here than in my home country and that I could make everyone proud. Back in Lebanon, I had a life of luxury, adventures, and partying. I was spoiled by my family and had everything I had ever asked for. But none of that gave me joy. I felt all of that was meaningless. So, I wanted to make something of myself; I wanted to make meaning out of my life.

Adjusting to a New Life in Dubai

Starting a new life in Dubai was not easy—especially after the lifestyle I'd had until then. Back home, most of my needs were tended to; here, I had to do everything by myself.

But I didn't complain. Instead, I looked at it as a transition from being a spoilt brat to becoming a real man. So, I took up the challenge and woke up the next day feeling pumped up for my new life in this land of opportunities.

Getting into Real Estate

I quickly started applying for jobs in real estate and started to get responses. I went to all of the companies I applied to, but none of them gave me a feeling that they were the right place for me to work. I was confident that when I found the right fit I would know right away, and I was right.

After a few other interviews, I walked into an interview for Provident Estate, which was one of the least luxurious branches of the industry. Most of the agents looked like gangsters—totally dishevelled, even intimidating. But I decided that this was where I wanted to work. After the interview, the director of the company offered me a job but asked me to get a brokerage license before I started. I then walked out of the office and broke down—not because I was shattered, but because it was the first time in my life where I had got what I really wanted instead of settling for what came my way.

So I immediately went to the Dubai Land Department and registered for the Brokerage License Certification. Since it was something I badly wanted, I decided to become a good student and attend all the classes—unlike my schooling days, when I spent most of the time whiling away the hours in the backbenches.

The instructor, Mrs Hiba Jabir, was someone who had come to Dubai in search of a new life and built a successful career. She was an ocean of knowledge and had incredible expertise on the subject. On the first day of class, she looked at me and said I would make it big in the industry. At that time, I was lost thinking about the reason behind why she had made that comment. I wondered if she was making fun of me, but maybe her expertise as an instructor enabled her to predict what kind of future I would have in this industry.

Early Days in the Job and Losing Motivation

Once the course was done, I took my exams and waited anxiously for the results. The hard work paid off and I got my brokerage license. I was on cloud nine! I then went back to the company to start working. Once I settled in at the new workplace, I observed how the other agents were pitching properties to the clients. I wondered how I could do it even better. I spent time reading articles on real estate, keeping track of news related to the industry, and even learning about the history of Dubai to understand the sales trends and other related information—this last one was especially important since I was new to the city. However, even with all this information, we were still one lost group made up of people who didn't know how to even get listings, let alone move them.

With time, I began to lose motivation. Nothing was working out, despite this being my dream job. Working long hours in the heat, using the metro, and barely having three meals a day wasn't really helping. So, I decided to quit the job and settle for a nine-to-five job, which would at least let me live a comfortable life.

AN INSPIRATIONAL MEETING WITH THE CEO

With resigning as my only thought in mind, I knocked on the CEO's door. I had never met him before, but under the circumstances, I thought it was best to hand him my resignation in person. I told him that I had run out of money and that I needed to look for a job that would pay me a salary to cover my expenses. Never in a million years could I have expected his reply. He told me that he wouldn't let me go because he saw a bright future for me with the firm. He said he believed in me and that he would be willing to invest in me.

As I stared at him in disbelief, he went on to talk about his humble beginnings: how he had moved to Dubai from the UK to start a new life, how he had worked hard and, with persistence, become the owner of a successful real estate company by the age of twenty-six. He had faced many hardships too. But he never quit. He'd weathered the storm so he could enjoy the rainbows that followed.

His story inspired me, and I decided not to leave. Instead, I would persevere until I saw the rainbows.

SECOND BEGINNINGS

After my chat with the CEO, there was a new fire of passion ignited in me. I wanted to prove myself. I sold off my phone and whatever jewellery I had at the pawnshop to help me with my expenses. I cut off all the negative people in my life and stayed in my zone, focusing on the only thing that mattered—succeeding in whatever I did.

Soon, I started to close rentals with different agents and made my first big paycheck—10,000 AED. Now that I had enough money for my food, travel, and other expenses, I could focus on how to be different from the thousands of other agents doing the same thing: calling the landlords, getting the listings, making sales, and so on …

So I did a bit of research on different types of real estate I could work in. Soon, I found out that the hotel apartment industry was practically untouched and had a lot of scope. But the real challenge there was to get those hotel apartments and make sure the commissions were safe. I took a leap of faith and walked into a hotel apartment building owned by a huge brand and asked to meet their sales director. The receptionist asked me if I had an appointment; I replied in the negative but told her that he would be interested in meeting me. I told her that I would wait until he had some free time. An hour passed, but the sales director still didn't come to see me. So I told the receptionist I wanted to rent two- or three-bedroom apartments and would like a tour of the place.

On seeing the apartments, I had the same feeling I had back when I went to the Provident Estate interview. I knew this was where I was going to make my money. So I decided to wait for the sales director, however long it took.

After two to three hours, I finally got to meet him. He greeted me with a smile, but when I told him I was a real estate agent, that smile faded. I tried to explain to him that I was not like the other agents, and after a long conversation, he asked me what my proposal was, listened to what I had to say, smiled politely, and left.

But I made a vow to myself—that I would get this place, and I would get it exclusively.

Now, getting one unit in Dubai itself was hard. How could I get 160 luxury apartments belonging to a huge brand? It seemed like an impossible feat. But I wasn't discouraged. I was determined. I went back to the office and brainstormed over how to make a proposal that he couldn't refuse. I researched a lot on how to make great proposals, working not only on the real estate aspects but also on my body language and personality. I knew that if I were to be successful, I would have to cover all the bases.

I went to the sales director with two proposals and returned with a rejection. But I was still determined. So, in my third proposal, I decided to *show* him how good I was instead of just telling him. I approached the security guards of all the surrounding buildings, paid them, and found out the available units in each building, along with the contact details of the landlords. Soon, I started to have three to four viewings per day. I made sure to take these people to the hotel apartments even though they wanted an unfurnished house, just to show them that I could bring them a lot of clients.

Soon, the staff of the hotel apartment building started to take notice and asked me why there were no closings despite the high number of viewings of the property. I simply told them that generating leads was my priority; although I could get up to ten clients each week, I wanted to keep it open to the market, unlike other agents who could only get two to three clients each week and were eager to close.

I then asked them to give me the property exclusively and said that I'd make the clients rain for them, and the director asked me to draft a proposal with whatever I wanted in it. Within a week, we closed the deal, and I finally had my first big success—just five months after moving to this city.

This not only transitioned my career but gave me even more confidence to close better and bigger deals. In a span of just a few months, I started closing multiple units a week; I also got my driver's license, rented a car, rented a great place, and furnished it according to my taste. I'd gone from being homesick in a new city to finally making it big; I could now feel proud of myself and my achievements.

By the second year, I managed to take over 1500 properties—exclusively. That's more than what 20 people can usually handle, but I liked working. Parties didn't mean anything to me anymore because I had found a new drive in life, and I was just chasing it.

GIVING IS BETTER

People usually don't know what they want, nor are they completely interested in what they do. That is why most of them get stuck in a spiral of confusion between whether to chase a dream or just stick to a secure job.

Millions of people move to new places every day armed with nothing but dreams and hopes of making it big. I was one of them, and with constant persistence, I managed to make it big. Now, I want to help others achieve their dreams, in whatever way I can.

If this book helps you—the reader—in any way, I hope that someday you might seek to help others like you; that's all I want.

GIVE YOUR EXPERTISE WITHOUT EXPECTATIONS

Always give your expertise, knowledge, and time to people, even if you know that it won't immediately lead to a business association. Once you leave a good/great impression, they will always remember you and send you referrals. You never know—one small act could lead to big things.

To illustrate my point, let me tell you a story about one of my clients. An Italian woman—about 55 years old—called me one afternoon asking for a viewing of a three-bedroom apartment. The call was short, and she agreed to meet at 3 pm. I showed her the property, then we grabbed a coffee and went down to the beach, where I got talking about my life and how I came to be here. Note that I always talk to clients like I am talking to friends; it breaks the ice and makes everyone comfortable—and it always leads to a great relationship.

So, three hours passed by with this client without any expectations regarding a deal; I was simply enjoying the conversation. I am talking about my life with her, and she is doing the same when she gets a call from her husband saying that he has finished work and is on his way to meet us.

Turns out, her husband is the CEO of a multi-billion-dollar European company and an honourable gentleman who later became a client and referred lots of his friends to me. It just goes to show that you get out what you put in; it pays to get to know people, to put in the effort and make conversation. And this is just one of many stories where I put a little time in and reaped great rewards.

I am writing this book to help millennials like you and me—people who dream big and have a passion to succeed in their lives—to take charge and secure their future through gaining returns in real estate. So, turn the page and start the journey with me as I share with you a secret formula—the Trinity of Success.

CHAPTER 2

THE AWAKENING

The first step to bringing about change is nourishing the soul.

First of all, I would like to congratulate you on purchasing this book. This is an indication that you want to change your life and become the best version of yourself. Basically, every change that happens is brought about by one decision; just taking things step by step and being consistent will lead you where you want to be. Many people fear change—it's human nature. The key to success is to embrace it, and this chapter will show you the first step.

The human body is magical—it can adapt. You can break any habit by taking a particular action consistently for 21 days. Let me give you an example here: a pack of cigarettes only has 20 cigarettes, not more, because smoking 21 would potentially lead to an addiction. This applies to everything in life when done on a consistent basis. So, in order for us to change, the first thing we need to do is understand and acknowledge the fact that where we are today is no one's fault—it's not the country, it's not your family, it's not your friends, it's not your culture.

Abandoning Misconceptions

To take the first steps towards building this best version of yourself, you need to let go of some common misconceptions. The following are commonly held beliefs that do nothing but hold you back—until you abandon them, nothing will change. Let's take a brief look at them.

Misconception #1: I need to be lucky to make it big in life. The most successful people—no matter where they are, what industry they're in, or how wealthy they are—have not made the big leagues simply because they're lucky. Nor are those who haven't succeeded simply unlucky. These people have made their dreams a reality because they were determined to do so. Nothing was going to get in their way. Success has nothing to do with luck—you simply get out what you put in.

Misconception #2: I need money to make money. Not true! You need courage to make money. Like many others before me, I took a huge gamble to get where I am today. I had to make sacrifices, and most of all, I had to believe in myself. It wasn't easy, and there were times when I feared I wouldn't succeed, but I was brave, and I never gave up, because I had a vision and nothing was going to stop me from getting there, especially not self-doubt.

Misconception #3: I need to live day by day and hope for the best. When I decided in that CEO's office that I was going to persevere, I knew I would have to come up with a plan. I thought about where I wanted to be and began to work out the steps I would need to take to get there. There were late nights, early mornings, and lots of Plan B's. The only way to get through is to plan ahead—you can't just wing it. Nothing comes down to chance; it's all about careful planning and setting goals.

You, and *only* you, are in charge of your life, and you should strive to become the best version of yourself in order to get to where you want to be, even if that means letting go of beliefs that absolve you of responsibility when things don't go the way you want them to. If you're not there already, you need to make a change. And for you to bring about this change, you need to start by taking care of your diet. And when I say 'diet', I don't only mean the food you eat, but the ideas you're thinking about, the surroundings you put yourself into—the things that feed the soul.

So, in this chapter, I am going to show you how to take care of your diet by breaking it down into the Trinity of Success, which involves sharpening the mind, sharpening the body, and sharpening the soul.

THE TRINITY OF SUCCESS

For me, learning and putting into practice the trinity of success was a major turning point. And I can tell you now, it really works. Think of your life as being divided into three areas: mind, body, and soul. For you to lead a successful, healthy, and happy life, you must establish a balance between these three elements. This is not a new concept, but it *is* one that will change your life. How do I know? Because it completely changed mine. Before I came to Dubai, I was living the party lifestyle; I had everything handed to me and no responsibilities. I didn't have to worry about goals or eating well—everything was about living in the moment and enjoying life. But when I came to Dubai, and things started becoming harder, I knew that something had to change. Before I discovered the trinity of success, I wasn't fulfilled; I didn't have the drive I do today. Now, I tell people every single day that it is the only way to get to where you want to be in life.

First, you feed your mind. You give yourself a sense of purpose. Then, you feed your body. This will give you the energy you need to fuel the other areas. Next, you nurture your soul; this will give you the strength to pursue your dreams. Just remember, you cannot focus on one or two areas alone—the trinity is threefold. For it to work, you must strike a balance between the three. Here's how you do that.

FOOD FOR THE MIND

There is a magical way in how our brains function—especially the subconscious part—when we write stuff on a piece of paper. It's not every day that we wake up in a state of mind where we just want to jump out of bed and go to work. But seeing our goals in front of us is a major booster, no matter what the circumstances are. Even if we're not feeling like we want to go meet people and network, seeing our goals in front of us works as a reminder of why we're going through all of this effort and why we need to change.

It's critical to know what we want from life—and not only what we need—in order to achieve greatness. Don't be afraid to aim high, because anything can be achieved. Let me give you an example of goals—they can be anything, from owning cars or a house to earning $10 million or $100 million, to having a beautiful family and stable life, etc. Whatever your goals are, write them down on a piece of paper and stick it somewhere where you can see it every day. When you wake up, they will be there, on your closet, on the wall, on your desk, and so on. No matter where you choose to stick your list, make sure that you see it every day, to remind yourself why you're putting in all this effort.

Now, let's sharpen our minds and seize that winning mindset! As hard as it might be for you to believe you are a winner, you are. The proof is right here in your hands—you have purchased this book and you're taking the time to read it and change your life. At the end of this chapter, you'll find a spot for you to begin drafting your goals; I want you to use this as a tool to get you thinking about what it is you want to achieve.

FOOD FOR THE BODY

When it comes to our body, we really need to sharpen the value and stay away from junk food. We need to stay away from bad sleeping habits and put ourselves on the right track. If we are engaging in habits that are counterproductive to our goals, we need to break them and seek out healthy ones. Each one of us has a different body type. Some need five hours of sleep, some need six or seven, and some even need eight hours of sleep. No matter what your case is, I want you to go to sleep before midnight and wake up before sunrise. I am sure all of us have heard the saying *the early bird gets the worm.* Just remember, you're not here to be the average bird—you are here to become the eagle.

Once you wake up, no matter how you feel, you must make your bed. This will be the first task or accomplishment of the day. And then you have to work out, whether you have a gym in your building or not. Go out, walk down the street for a minimum of 30 minutes. Sweat it out—this will give you an amazing feeling and give you an energy boost that will last you the entire day.

This must be done constantly for 21 days; after that, your body will start telling you, *I need to work out.* Processed food and sugars will make your body tired. They will only make you feel lazy and sleepy. They might taste good, but they're poisonous, so stay away from them as much as possible.

Lastly, make sure you are drinking two litres of water every day. Ensure you are getting enough fruits and vegetables—and stay away from fried foods. You can have one 'cheat meal' per week to reward yourself.

FOOD FOR THE SOUL

Your surroundings are very important because they have a direct effect on your mindset. So I want you to keep yourself away from the negative people who poison your life, whether they are colleagues, friends, or even family. If you are wondering how to spot these people, let me help you. Negative people:

- are always angry
- are ungrateful
- always have negative comments or something bad to say about you and others
- talk about other people all the time, and
- are always nosy and want to know what everyone's business is, even though it's none of their business.

The more you can stay away from these kinds of people, the better things will be for you. When they see that you are learning to be better, they will bring you down by saying things like: "This is all fake, and it's impossible for you to make it."

Only a few people in life are awakened enough to be able to surround themselves with like-minded people, or at least people on the same mission in life as themselves. But a really good start is eliminating those who are in direct opposition to what you are trying to achieve—those people who want nothing more than to see you fail.

Now we have covered the diet for your mind, body, and soul. Let us now get started with the fundamentals of real estate, the first of which is prospecting. Are you ready? If so, just turn to the next chapter.

MY GOALS

Use this page to plan out some goals. Remember, goals can change; you can revise these at any time. This is just a starting point. Your goals might get bigger or take a different direction than you thought when you first set out, and that's okay.

WHY HAVE YOU CHOSEN THIS INDUSTRY?

WHAT WOULD YOU LIKE TO ACHIEVE IN THIS INDUSTRY?
Short term (3 months):
Medium term (6 months):
Long term (12 months):

CHAPTER 3
PROSPECTING

The more hands you shake, the more money you make.

By the end of this chapter, you will know how to approach people successfully. I'm going to introduce you to all the different ways of prospecting, which plays a really important role in securing successful real estate deals; in fact, it covers almost 50% of the job.

First, I'm going to tell you how I met my biggest client by far in my six years in this industry. The story goes like this: I was invited to a social event; I wasn't really feeling like going or talking to the people there, but my friends were really pushing me. So I managed to force myself to get up and go to the event. I dressed properly; I got myself some business cards; I went over there, and we started meeting people. Suddenly, I heard someone behind me speaking the language of my home country: pure Lebanese Arabic. I turned around to see who it was—and guess what? This guy was from a city close to mine. So, we started talking, and he asked me what I did for a living. I told him that I was into real estate and informed him about the type of services I provide. We then exchanged numbers, and I haven't heard from him since.

But after a month, I got a phone call from someone. He introduced himself to me and told me that he had got my number from that guy I met at that event, and he also expressed his wish to meet me. Since then, we've done a huge number of sales; we've also built up his portfolio—and oh boy, have I been blessed ever since.

It was then that I really understood the importance of joining in and attending events, because at each one, every person is a potential buyer, and you don't want to be missing out on going to places and meeting people like that. You need to get out there—have that conversation, connect with people, and increase your reach in order to be successful in this industry. We call this 'prospecting'. So, what are the types of prospecting, and how do we do it?

DIFFERENT TYPES OF PROSPECTING

There are five mediums of prospecting:

- Social networking events
- Phone calls, or what we call 'cold calling'
- WhatsApp messages, or what we call 'cold texting'
- Emails
- Digital media

Let us now delve into each of these in detail.

SOCIAL NETWORKING EVENTS

Social networking events happen every week, mostly on weekends. It can be an art gallery show, it can be a business gathering; it can be about banking, finances, or anything else. Also, it can happen anywhere in the country. At all these social networking events, there will be people from multiple industries—contractors, developers, salespeople, insurance people, and so on.

What you need to do is to join that event. And always, always, rule number one—keep a huge smile on your face. Never forget to pack your business cards; you don't know who you are about to meet. At events, be sure to talk to people, ask questions as much as possible, and be friendly. Don't do it for the sake of bringing in more business. Try to understand people's needs and problems so you can better understand what you can offer them in terms of a solution.

It's very important to do that as much as possible, and to make a great first impression so that people remember you as someone who is well-presented, well-dressed, well-spoken, polite, and friendly; try to make yourself known as someone they can count on.

COLD CALLING

Lots of people misuse this method of prospecting by just calling people at random and saying things like "Hey, I'm calling to find out if you want to buy/you want to sell/you want to do this ...." Don't be this person; this is why most people hate cold calling. However, this can change if you have something nice to offer.

Let's say you are calling databases of landlords in a specific building. Don't start with "Hi, I'm calling you to see if you want to rent or sell your house." Instead, do your homework by approaching the building, talking to the security guards, and finding out which apartments are vacant. And once you know which ones are vacant, call the landlord. Say "Hi. I was in the building today showing a very nice couple an apartment similar to yours, with the same view but on a lower floor. They love it and can't wait to move in. I'm just wondering if you would like to rent out your apartment too, and if so, what price would you be looking for?" This landlord will listen to you because he knows that you already have an offer and that you already have business coming in; straight away, he is more likely to treat you with respect. He will not be annoyed by your phone call because you're simply asking him if he has something ready to sell or lease. Not only that, but you're already familiar with the building, which better places you to find tenants or buyers. Once you have more than one landlord in one building, you will get more and more and more listings, which means more business.

Cold texting

It's very important to know how to text a prospective client. Everyone can say hi to someone, and everyone can send a long paragraph that no one wants to read. When it comes to cold texting, make sure you send the same content that you would by phone, but send it on WhatsApp, addressing the person by name. For example:

> *Hey Eric, it's Anthony. I was in the building today with this beautiful couple who saw an apartment just like yours. They loved it and can't wait to move in. I'm looking for other available apartments and can offer you the same parameters I offered the owner of this apartment.*

You could even offer a brief introduction, outlining your achievements and industry experience to boost your credibility. This lets the client know you are different; you're not just any agent in the market, you're an expert. WhatsApp can also be used to upload your portfolio and brochures or to direct the receiver to your social media pages for more information.

EMAILS

Emails are even more informative. Just remember to make sure that you include your signature at the bottom, showing your name and your credentials. This will let the recipient know which company is contacting them.

Again, you can boost your credibility by outlining your achievements and industry experience; just be wary of boring the recipient with too many details. Feel free to include pictures to make your email more eye-catching. And if you feel like your writing is lacking impact, you can always hire a copywriter or a content creator to help you.

DIGITAL MEDIA

The last method involves the use of digital media. Nowadays, people are more into visuals. They like to see something tangible in front of them. The best way to reach these people is through video content. All you have to do is pick up your phone, open the camera, and record your message. Let's say you sent your client a WhatsApp text, and they never answered you. Or you made a phone call or sent an email, but you never heard back from them—this means that digital media will be your method.

The script can pretty much be the same as you would write in a text message or email; start off by addressing them personally—and remember to keep it short and sweet. Once they see the video, believe me, they will reply, even if they're not interested in doing business or they have nothing available for sale or rent. This is because they will feel that you have customised your message for them, and they must give you the courtesy of acknowledging that. I've used this method and it works for me like magic.

Remember, it's very important for you to have a Facebook page, Instagram page, and YouTube page. You need to make sure all bases are covered; as with all things, everyone has their preferences when it comes to social media. If you want to be successful, you will need to make sure that you can be located on a variety of platforms so you're able to connect with all potential clients. We'll talk more about the individual social media platforms later on, but for now, recognise that in today's climate, social media is an essential tool for success. For more ideas on using digital and social media, see my podcasts and my online academy, the details of which you'll find at the end of this book.

WHY IS PROSPECTING SO IMPORTANT?

Before we move on, I would like to tell you a few stories about prospecting. Naturally, there are unlimited stories involving prospecting—it happens every day. I still recall one of these stories very well. I called someone, and no sooner had I mentioned my name and explained that I was calling him for a particular purpose than the guy immediately hung up the phone. Soon after, he called me back, and he's like, "Are you the same Anthony that has a very big profile on Instagram? And you just did this sale?" He then said, "Oh, I do apologise. I thought you were gonna be one of those annoying agents! I've heard about you; you are all over social media. And yes, I would love to meet with you and would love to give you all of my portfolio to manage."

This guy had over 25 units, and now I had this business secured. That's the power of social media: this guy already knew about me without me even saying a word.

The other story I want to tell you belongs to my colleague. He was trying really hard to approach someone on WhatsApp, but the guy wasn't answering. He came to know that this person would be at a social networking event, so he decided to go there and wait for him to appear. Eventually, they bumped into each other, and he said, "I tried approaching you in every possible way. You left me no choice but to crash this party in order to talk to you." And this person found that very humorous. I think he might have been impressed that my friend went to such lengths to meet him, but it was all worth it in the end, because you know what? They ended up closing over $15 million worth of sales together.

There are tons of good prospecting stories I can tell you, but let's leave it at that for now. The moral of these stories is that prospecting is 50% of the job. And when you prospect with all your heart, you achieve success. Just remember to always keep a smile on your face, have the right attitude, and no matter what the objection is, know how to handle it.

So, to summarise this chapter for you, never forget the importance of prospecting, and keep practising! The more you try, the better the outcome. Eventually, everything will become easier and you will become a professional prospector. Yes, your first call will be hard. But the second one will be easier, and the third one easier still. For the first call of the day, make sure you call someone you already know as a form of a warm-up exercise; then later on, you can start calling strangers as you build up your confidence and find your rhythm.

Listen, guys, no one is here to judge you or tell you that you're no good; you just need to find your character. Even if you are shy about talking in front of the camera, you should tell yourself that no one's opinion matters, and at the end of the day, you cannot pay bills using anyone's opinion. So rehearse well and *try*—because no one was born knowing it all. We've all got to learn through trial and error, no matter what industry we're in. So keep trying, keep training, and you too can become the best of the best. And now, let's move on to the next chapter, where I'm going to teach you how to find people online and get them to approach you.

CHAPTER 4
GETTING THE LISTINGS

Seeing is believing.

As I mentioned earlier, prospecting comprises 50% of the business; the remaining 50% is the listings. In this chapter, you will learn how to secure listings using a variety of different channels and methods.

Have you ever wondered why your colleague is getting so many calls, or why a certain person is so successful, and another person is not? Well, it all comes down to listings. Let me tell you why listings are so essential to our business.

Once you get the listings, whether sole listings, exclusive listings, or multi-listings, this will boost your exposure.

So, whenever people are searching for homes, you will pop up. There are lots of channels to get listings, including databases, SMS alerts, security guards, facility management, word of mouth, and once again, the ever-useful social media. We'll cover each of these shortly.

Let me first tell you about the two types of listings. The first is the exclusive listing—the landlord gives you, and only you, his property to sell or manage for a period of up to 90 days; once those 90 days have lapsed, he is allowed to pass the listing on to others. So whether the client has approached you directly or has come through another agent, you will always be entitled to your commission. For this reason, the exclusive listing is very important. However, landlords are sceptical about giving an agent an exclusive listing if they don't know them. Instead, they will give it to multiple people, and whoever closes the deal first will be entitled to the full commission; this is known as a multi-listing.

Now that we're familiar with the types of listings, we're ready to explore how we secure those listings. The first way we can go about it is through the use of databases.

DATABASES

So, when I talk about databases, I mean making the most of building databases. What you need to do first is make sure that you are specialised in an area and a specific building—then you call landlords in that area and start building up your contact list. When I say "specialised", I mean you have learned the real estate history of the area. You have to learn the history of all transactions in the last three years and, most importantly, you need to know the nearest schools, hospitals, laundry, pharmacy and nursery, and methods of public transportation. Most of the people coming to you will be asking you the same questions. Only when you know the answers to these questions and have decided on your approach, will you be regarded as a credible agent and secure the listing. And who knows, the landlord might even give it to you on an exclusive basis.

On top of area knowledge, you need to know the building and unit types so you can start building your inventory of available properties. This might sound hard for a beginner, but in fact, it is not. And once you do it properly, life becomes easier and more enjoyable.

Every agent uses calling databases to determine whether a listing is available. These databases exist for every property and contain the owner's contact details, making it easy for you to get in touch with them. However, many landlords will receive phone calls from agents four or five times a day, which becomes very annoying for them. So saying things like, "We've been through the building with this person and they have already given me an offer; if you like, I can liaise with them regarding your unit and get the ball rolling" can really set your call apart from the others.

SMS ALERTS

SMS alerts are texts you send out for a specific purpose; this may be anything from securing potential listings to reaching buyers. For example, you may send out an SMS blast to the residents of an apartment building to determine if anyone wants to sell or lease their apartment, or you may contact buyers to let them know when an apartment has become available. Although the SMS itself should be short, you can always use a link to direct the receiver to a location where they'll find more information—for example, to a landing page. In your SMS alert, you should advise the recipient that you are the area specialist. When they click on the link, it will redirect them to your page, where they can see who you are, what you have done, and everything about the listing.

Security guards

Every building has a security guard. And this guard has all the data pertaining to the building because landlords must give them their details in case of an emergency. All you have to do is become friends with the guard and make a business deal with them by offering a referral fee on every client they send your way. Lots of people approach buildings without an appointment and say something like, "We are looking to move in here, who do you recommend we speak to?" If this guard knows that referring them to you will make him money, you will have secured yourself a verified source of genuine leads.

Facility management

Facility management has access to all the databases of the community they deal with on a day-to-day basis.

Landlords will tell them, "I'm not gonna renew the contract, I'm getting out of the property, I want to sell it." They can feed you information and verify it. As with security, making a deal with them regarding a referral fee will place you at an enormous advantage.

Word of Mouth

Word of mouth is essential in this business. You should always encourage clients to refer you to their friends; they will always remember you if you give them perfect service. Whenever someone wants to do something to do with real estate, or knows someone who does, they will remember you as the person who helped them last time. Once you have listed multiple units in a specific building, all the landlords will start to regard you as their number one contact when new listings become available.

Social Media

You should always be thinking about content for social media. Think videos on your YouTube, on your Facebook, on your LinkedIn—on your everywhere—saying what you have done and showing you shaking hands with clients and closing deals. Always ask your clients to give you some type of review, whether handwritten or posted on Google; the latter, in particular, will give you added credibility.

As your social media profile gains momentum, the landlords themselves will start to call you and ask you to work on their apartments. And from there, it all gets easy! Your phone will be ringing off the hook, so to speak, with requests for you to arrange viewings and close more deals.

Covering All Bases

You need to understand that using one or two methods, or even three methods, is fine. But if you want to really publicise the excellent service you provide and you want to be the person getting the stock, you need to use *all* of these methods. Once you have 35 listings on the portal, you are deemed an area specialist. This will bring with it huge exposure and your phone will not stop ringing.

There have been many times when people have called me to rent an apartment, but after meeting me face to face, instead of renting a studio or a one-bedroom, I'd convinced them to buy three-bedroom or four-bedroom townhouses. So never underestimate the power of a listing. Each and every one has the potential to be a great opportunity and a window forward.

In summary, once you have done your prospecting and are getting listings, you have covered nearly 100% of the actual world of work. Now, I want to take you on the journey of what to do next. In the next chapter, I'm going to talk you through a major step towards building a successful business, which is knowing how to manage your time.

CHAPTER 5

TIME MANAGEMENT

To get ahead, you must use your time wisely.

Knowing how to handle your time and organise yourself will change your life. And this will set you apart from the rest. So, in this chapter, you are going to learn how to manage your time and optimise your day, as time is one of the most valuable assets available to you.

Time management is a skill possessed by the 1% on the planet who have found the true key to success. And once we see how this 1% use their time, comparing it to the 99% who just want to waste time or kill time, we can clearly understand the difference between the two. We all have only 24 hours a day; it is how we utilise time that makes us different, and it's what helps us achieve better outcomes and better incomes.

Let me ask you a question: we always look at the 20% that produce big money and we wonder, *What do they have that the rest of us don't?* Well, the answer is that this 20% of people want to outwork everyone. And when I say outwork, it means they put in more effort and more time.

Let me give you an example. The average employee works from nine to six. This employee might wake up at 8 am, rush to the toilet, have his shower, get dressed, drive to work, and work until noon. At noon, he might have his lunch break and then return to work (often, with no energy) and will wait until 6 pm rolls around and he gets to leave. Then he might go back home, chill on his sofa for a bit and watch television or meet up with his friends to have a drink, then come back, eat, sleep, and so on. And that's it—that's all his life is.

Every day, we look at this person and we see him being unproductive, killing time. In all likelihood, his lifestyle isn't healthy at all. And it shows on his face, and in his behaviour and his character. He is not a happy person.

So, what to do? Let me now tell you the best way of dividing up the day in order for us to make it perfect. At the end of this chapter is a chart I use. You can duplicate it and use it yourself or you can come up with your own—it's all up to you. What really matters here is the first task of the day, which consists of the time you wake up and the time you go to bed. The rest is up to you to customise and make productive on your own.

So now we draw a chart. Let's say you are used to waking up at 6 am. I always emphasise the benefits of waking up at 6 am. Why? Let's say most people wake up at 8 am and go to work at 9 am. Waking up at 6 am gives you an extra two to three hours over the rest. With these two hours, you can put in more work and more effort. And trust me, it adds up! This comes to a total of 576 hours per year. That's nearly 600 extra hours you can use to outshine everyone.

So waking up early is something sacred. Believe me, guys, I don't like it. I don't want to wake up early. But after doing it for more than 21 days, as we talked about earlier, your body can adapt to any habit. After waking up, I will go straight to the gym at 6:15 and be back at home at 7 am. Then I have a shower and get dressed for work. I will arrive at the office between 7:30 and 7:45, depending on the traffic. At 8 am I will be doing my first task, which is updating myself on the market trends and the latest news, both locally and internationally. It's very important to follow the local and international news so we can see what's happening in the market—especially if you are working in a city like Dubai, where there is a huge variety of nationalities and anything can happen; for example, good news in Europe could mean good or bad news for us. Once you know what's been happening in the stock market or with gold and silver or crude oil, you'll have an indication of who is making money right now and who you should be targeting immediately, or who might be losing out a little bit because of an event in their area.

Okay, so the first task, as we said, is update yourself on the market trends and the latest news—done. The second one, which is sending out emails, will be at 8:30. Then, I work on the list of prospects I reach out to daily. This happens from 9:30 until 12:30. I'll be calling these people and maximising my time by attempting to arrange meetings with them in the afternoon, because at end of the day, if you spend all of your time in the office instead of meeting people face to face, you will not be able to do business.

I'll then take my lunch break between 12:30 and 1 pm. Once lunch is over, I reconfirm the meeting times and locations in writing; for example: *Mr X, it was lovely talking to you, just confirming that we're meeting* ... This is also a good time to submit documents and complete other relevant paperwork.

By this time, I'll also be doing the SMS blast, as discussed earlier. So, let's say from around 3:30 to 8 pm, I will be conducting viewings, meeting people, and trying to close deals. Once I finish at 8 pm, I'll head back home.

As I'm driving home—and I do this on a daily basis—I listen to podcasts, mostly because they are a brain opener. Podcasts are full of ideas I can utilise. Once I reach home at 8:30, I have my dinner and relax a little bit. I take a shower and put on some comfortable clothes. Then, at 10 pm, I prepare my social media content. I prepare the basics—I don't try to plan out full scripts; I just put in some dot points. For example, I might make note of something that happened to me that day that is worth making a video about. I even talk about experiences I have had with my clients, or anything I can put on social media that will be interesting and productive for my followers. I'll talk more about the power of social media and how to work it to your advantage in the next chapter. Last but not least, by 11 pm I head off to bed, and just before I fall asleep, I ask myself, "Was I productive today? How did I maximise my chances of becoming the best person I can be? What have I done right? What have I done wrong?"

This is a helpful assessment that you can undertake on a daily, weekly, monthly, and eventually yearly basis.

NOW IT'S YOUR TURN

Now that you know how I've divided up my daily activities, I want you to fill out a chart for yourself. You can use the template on the next page or design one of your own—it's entirely up to you. Remember, it's very important to wake up early, work out, and get to sleep before midnight. Other than that, how you want to divide up your day to maximise your productivity is up to you. Once you've finished, put your chart somewhere you can see it from now on. This will become your new habit; this will be what you're going to be doing on a daily basis until your body adapts to these changes.

DAILY SCHEDULE

TIME	ACTIVITY
6 AM	
7 AM	
8 AM	
9 AM	
10 AM	
11 AM	
12 PM	
1 PM	
2 PM	
3 PM	
4 PM	
5 PM	
6 PM	
7 PM	
8 PM	
9 PM	
10 PM	
11 PM	

CHAPTER 6
SOCIAL MEDIA

The 21st century: Where your clients can get to know you without ever actually having to meet you.

In this chapter, I'm going to teach you how to utilise your social media to the maximum while using multiple applications to give yourself huge exposure. This way, people will start to get to know who you are and what you do; it will also allow them to approach you, instead of you chasing them.

Social media is the most powerful tool of the 21st century. We are extremely lucky to be alive in this era, where all of us are connected, and we are just one click away from each other. Back in the day, if people wanted to meet each other, they would just speak on the phone once or twice. If they had an appointment with someone who lived in a different country, they had to fly there to have a meeting—and most of those meetings were terrible because there was no business contact, and it became an absolute waste of time, resources, and money.

It's safe to say that social media came in and changed all of that. For example, nowadays, if I want to reach anyone, I can simply log into Facebook, YouTube, LinkedIn, or Instagram and reach out to them by sending them a text message, or even an interesting voice note. Often, I can even check whether they've read it or not. And once they read or listen to the message, they think, "Oh, I should reply to this person. Maybe there's something interesting in it for me." And that's how people get connected. As a matter of fact, I now have thousands of contacts all over the planet, people with whom I do business but have not yet met face to face. This is mostly due to the series of lockdowns we've experienced as a result of the COVID-19 pandemic. We speak on a daily basis by sending videos, having Zoom calls, and using the many social media tools we have at our disposal. And, again, we've never even met each other—which is something magical.

The most used application in the world is Facebook; it has over 2.1 billion users—and they are active users who use it on a daily basis. Number two is Instagram, which has 1.4 billion active users. Third place goes to LinkedIn, which has over 800 million users, and all of these users mainly use it for business purposes; you don't see them posting family pictures or posting a day out with their family on this social platform. LinkedIn is mostly about their services—what they do and the people they interact with. So this is an extremely important application for us to use in the real estate business. Number four is YouTube, where we are witnessing the phenomenon of *Seeing is Believing.* YouTube helps lots of people showcase their property and get the attention of buyers. Number five, which is a new but widely used application, is Zoom, a form of videoconferencing software. Now, let's speak about those one by one.

FACEBOOK

The beauty of Facebook is that it has the greatest number of users on the planet. It allows us to post pictures and videos, but also maintain landing pages or

Facebook pages where you can market your business. It's sort of like your own website, where you can post your working hours, your activities, your location, and everything related to you and your business—even your VAT registration number. You can tailor your posts to work like advertisements. It's also possible to link it to your personal account so that people can view your personal page. Then they can send requests to follow you and, once approved, they can follow everything you have been doing.

Another amazing thing about this application is that it's totally free; you don't have to pay anything for it. However, if you wish to maximise your exposure, you can learn how to work the Facebook Ads Manager; this way, you can handle your advertisements. You can target certain audiences by choosing the right age, location, and interests of your target audience, and they will then start seeing your advertisements and sending you inquiries. Also, you will be just one click away! Just drop them a message, such as, "Thank you, I've received your inquiry, how can I help you?" and you're good to go!

So it's extremely important to be on Facebook—it's an amazing tool for business, and it's the future. So, if you're not on it already, I urge you to open an account right now.

Instagram

The most-used social media application after Facebook is Instagram, which has become very popular since 2015. On Instagram, everyone showcases what they do in terms of business. Lately, we have seen a rise in people who call themselves 'social media marketers' and 'graphic designers'. They offer to customise your posts and make them interesting by following the psychology of fonts, font size, and font colour, bearing in mind how interaction occurs with certain fonts. As an example, let's think about the Netflix logo. It looks nice at first glance. But what's really interesting about it is the use of the colour red, which prompts the brain to become intrigued about what the owner of the logo has to offer. By comparison, Samsung has used the colour blue for its logo. Blue symbolises confidence, and confidence in turn symbolises credibility. And if you look at the McDonald's logo, you see the familiar mix of yellow and red—bright colours that stimulate the brain and send the signal that you should be eating here.

All these techniques are used all over social media, especially on Instagram. There's a lot of people who can help you do that and at very affordable prices; they can help you create the content and post it at the right time to get the highest engagement. Remember, there is a time difference from one country to another, as well as a difference in the level of engagement between audiences. When it comes to Dubai, the best posting time will always be between 4 am and 8 am. That's when most of your PRs will be on their phones, using social media actively.

Another thing about Instagram is that you can advertise through your stories. In them, you can also share links to your videos, articles, blogs—whatever you like. Instagram allows the same advertising as Facebook. As a matter of fact, you can connect Instagram and Facebook, and once you run an ad on Facebook, it will be shown on both Facebook and Instagram; in addition, when you do Instagram ads, they will run through your feed and through your story, both of which have massive reach.

LinkedIn

As I mentioned before, LinkedIn is an even easier way to get clients. This is because LinkedIn's reach is very high (way better than Instagram and Facebook). On LinkedIn, everyone writes their own bio, and you can see other people's profiles before you become friends. So let's say you're looking for people working at Sony—all you have to do is put this into the search bar, which will then present you with a list of people who have this listed as their main role. You can reach out to them by sending them a message. You can even send them a video introducing yourself and explaining why you'd like to get in touch. This is a very credible and appropriate way to connect with people on a professional level. LinkedIn users expect to receive requests or messages related to business, not just friendly messages.

The way I see it, your LinkedIn account should act like your CV, and you have to customise it and beautify it so you can make the most of it. You should never post anything on LinkedIn that you wouldn't like a prospective employer to see. Being a professional platform, it's not designed to showcase pictures of you at the beach or on holiday (unless, of course, you're a professional surfer or holiday tour guide); instead, you should be presenting yourself in a professional light, showcasing who you are when you're at work and what you can offer people in a professional capacity. Remember also that LinkedIn can provide endorsements; if you've worked at a particular company or organisation, this can be listed and fact-checked by anyone who is viewing your profile.

YOUTUBE

YouTube is the most-watched and most-used video application out of all of them. People spend hours and hours a day using YouTube without even realising it because of how easy it is to use the platform. And now they've introduced YouTube studios, where they teach everyone how to make a channel for themselves and start putting out content. All you need is one viral video for everyone to start following you.

On YouTube, you can make videos of up to 15 minutes without having any issues with uploading them. Should you need to, you can even upgrade your account, which enables you to make videos an hour or two long. You can upload podcasts, do interviews, showcase properties, and talk about your professional vision. Personally, I like to use it to capture anecdotes about the work I do; it's a great opportunity to share your success stories and talk about how you came to be where you are now, plus it's far more personal than a typed social media post.

If you want to have clients, if you want to have buyers, and if you want to ensure the best filtration of clients, YouTube is your go-to application.

ZOOM

Zoom is an amazing way for people to do business, especially if they are in different countries, or are too far away from each other to be meet in person. Zoom has fantastic video and sound quality. Calls can be between two people or a huge group, in which case someone will host the meeting and invite other people to join. Let me give you an example. Suppose I want to sell a property to a family—the husband and wife are in France, and the kids are at boarding school in Italy. All we have to do is agree on a time; then I'll send them the link to join the call through the Zoom app. Once everyone has joined the call, I can start sharing my main page. I can show them pictures and video footage of the property, all while talking them through the features of the property. This way, I am creating a group viewing without even seeing the people face to face. The best part is, I'm doing it all remotely and I don't even have to leave the office! Using this tool, I secured over 65 sales last year, and it was the first time I had used Zoom in my entire life. All this shows you the importance and power of social media.

Conquering Your Fear of the Camera

Now maybe lots of you will say, "But how can I be in front of a camera? I'm shy. What will people say about me?" I too had these thoughts in my head until I reached a point where I told myself, "You are the only one that is responsible for paying your bills and setting up your life." Essentially, other people's opinions do not pay your bills. You, and you alone, are responsible for paying your way through life. I knew I had to take control of my career—and to do this, I knew I needed to abandon my fear of making a fool of myself in front of the camera.

So I started doing videos. And believe me, my first video was terrible. But I put my vanity aside and kept it online as a reminder of just how far I have come. The second video was a little better. The third was even better, and eventually, when I got to the fifth and the sixth and the seventh, they all turned out to be amazing—from then, nothing could stop me. Today, I can do about ten videos a day. I don't even need to write a script. I just open my phone and start talking.

I want to introduce you to a simple technique that will make you more comfortable being in front of the camera. Every night, before going to bed, lots of people write in their diaries. They take a pen and a notebook and they start writing about how their day was. What I want you to do is ditch the pen and notebook and pick up the phone. It's just you and your phone and the empty room. Record yourself talking about how your day was.

You should do this on a daily basis. Remember, this is for your eyes only. It's just like a diary but in video form. Over time, you'll start to feel more comfortable talking to the camera; after a while, you won't even think about it. And that's when you're ready to take the next step and start recording content for your social media pages.

My advice? Just be yourself and put out content—no matter what imperfections you see in your videos, they are valuable because you give them value, and people everywhere want the information they contain. I am sure lots of people are sick and tired of seeing meaningless videos; they want *value* and they want knowledge, because at the end of the day, it's the 21st century. Knowledge and value are the new currency.

EMBRACE TECHNOLOGY

Before we end the chapter, I want to emphasise once again that social media is the future. You have to be there. If you're not there, now is the best time for you to put yourself there so you don't miss out on potential opportunities. Get on all of these applications and start putting out content. A single video can be used on YouTube, LinkedIn, Instagram, and Facebook. It's not that hard; once you're experienced, it will only take an additional ten or fifteen minutes out of your day to make one video. These tools have changed my life and I'm sure they will change yours. So, get on the wagon—I wish you the best of luck. Now that we have covered all the social media platforms, I'm going to talk about client types and how to handle each one.

CHAPTER 7

TYPES OF CLIENTS

A successful agent will handle hundreds of clients–what's important is to differentiate between them and determine how to handle them on an individual basis.

In this chapter, I'm going to introduce you to the different types of clients you will be encountering and how to handle them, one by one. There is a huge difference between a tenant, an end user-buyer, and an investor-buyer for residential properties. There's also a difference between business owners who want to buy offices and investors who want to purchase commercial properties. Knowing how to cater to their individual needs and preferences is what will set you aside from other agents and secure you the most listings. Let's get started!

Short-term Tenants

The first client you will be encountering is the short-term tenants. Basically, these are people who come to Dubai for a specific period of time, which can be anywhere from a month to two months, or even three months or more. They are not here on a contract; they're just looking to rent short-term properties. These people will not give you a hard time at all because they will be approaching you after seeing your listings. Once they see the property, they will come and check it out, give you their passports, sign a lease for a month or two, and that's it. But make sure you satisfy these people, answer all their questions, and give them what they need. Tell them where the nearest hospital is and let them know where the nearest landmarks are. If they are young people, they might be looking for nice restaurants, so recommend some nice places they can visit during their time here—they'll appreciate the extra effort you've put in to make them feel welcome.

Yearly tenants

The second type of client is the yearly tenant. These are the ones who live and work in Dubai, and they're looking for homes. They may be single people, a married couple, or even a big family. No matter what the case is, make sure you find them the best property. Always stay in touch with them—give them a call every two or three months to make sure everything is fine and ask them if they need anything else.

These tenants usually have friends in Dubai, which means they're very important for word-of-mouth advertising. If they're happy with your services, they'll refer their friends and acquaintances to you; when people come to visit them at their home and say they like it, these clients will drop your name as the person who located it. These clients will automatically be recommending you as the agent specialising in that area and the best-placed person to help them. So it's very important to maintain an amazing relationship with these tenants, because they are a very good source of referrals and, later on down the line, may even become buyers. And when they think about buying a property, of course, you want them to contact you first!

Now, let's talk about the types of buyers—the end users and investors.

End users

An end user is a client buying a property to live in. Usually, these buyers come single or as a family, so it's very important to understand their needs and requirements. Every buyer is looking for something different. Some want to be in a vibrant area next to the beach and others are looking for a family-oriented area next to a golf course, community facilities, or greeneries, etc.

In the case of a married couple, be sure to fulfil the wife's requirements—if she's happy with everything she's seeing, then a sale is guaranteed. Usually, wives are really focused on having nice kitchens and big living areas where they can enjoy time with their family or friends. And if she's looking for a view, give her the view she wants. If she's looking for a townhouse or a villa, then be sure to give her a proper backyard where she can spend time with her loved ones. Younger women might be focused on having a large bathroom with good lighting and plenty of drawer space—if that's the case, make sure you present them with something that's going to make them say "Wow, this is perfect!" Once you show her that special feature she has been looking for, that's it—you've sealed the deal.

Recently, a friend of mine closed a big deal amounting to around 45 million dollars. It was a huge deal—and they went way over budget. The place the buyers ended up with was far beyond anything they had originally anticipated. I couldn't believe it at first. That was, I couldn't believe it until my friend mentioned that a wife was involved. Then I immediately understood! My friend said that he could see the determination in her eyes while they were looking at the penthouse; she just had this look about her, like *If my husband doesn't buy this house for me, I am going to kill you.* She was going to get this apartment, no matter what. Here's a valuable lesson for you: the wife always wins. If you can find something she likes, you'll have yourself a sale.

INVESTORS

On the other hand, handling investors is a totally different game, one requiring a completely different approach, as they will only be looking for the ROI (Return on Investment—what they will be getting on a yearly basis due to an invested amount). So it is extremely important to be an area specialist who can tell them the history of the area or the transacted properties in the last three years. Most importantly, investors need to know about the nearby schools, hospitals, laundries, pharmacies, nurseries, and transportation facilities.

Remember, investors are only interested in figures and numbers. For example, an investor will tell you they are going to invest a million dollars and are looking for a six to eight per cent return per year. Once they own the property, they won't even really need to see it because, as an investor, they're only buying the numbers, not the property. Dubai attracts lots of international investors because it allows them to leverage their money through the post-handover payments plan, where a client needs to pay only 40% to 50% of the property amount to get his keys. The remaining 50% can be paid over three years. After they get the keys, the investor rents the property out to generate income from tenants, leveraging their money—and that's why they are so interested in this city.

There are other types of investment buyers looking into commercial properties. Some may be looking to purchase hotel apartments, which makes them similar to those seeking residential apartments. The only difference is that hotel apartments come fully furnished and will have services such as housekeeping. The unit will also include all bills, such as water, electricity, Wi-Fi, etc. The different types of commercial real estate can be vast and may include land or warehouses—basically any type of place where a business can be established. We often see people investing in offices and big commercial areas; they will either open their own business to save on rent or hold onto these properties, knowing that they're in a hot area and the demand will increase significantly later on.

So, what's really important is to remember that there are three essential tasks you need to perform: First is qualifying the client—understanding their exact needs and requirements—because you don't want to be pitching properties in which they have no interest. Second is fulfilling their needs from A to Z—you will find them the perfect property and they will decide they want to go ahead with it. And third, always put yourself in the shoes of the client.

A good technique, particularly when it comes to the latter, is to ask yourself: *Is this the way I would want my parents to be treated?* People everywhere, from all different cultures and walks of life, revere their parents. And why wouldn't they? After all, their parents raised them, looked after them, taught them all about life. That is why I say you should treat your clients in the same way you would want your parents to be treated. Integrity is everything. Give them the very best; make sure you are honest and that you listen to their needs and help them to the very best of your abilities. This will allow you to create a strong and successful relationship with these clients that can go on to become a beautiful friendship.

Essentially, you want your clients to become like extended family members—people you can count on and who can count on you in turn. To make this happen, you need to treat people with the same respect you show towards your parents—both your mother and your father. You need to implement full transparency, full honesty, and care towards your clients; by doing this, you are guaranteed to secure these clients for a lifetime. With that circle of trust comes a desire to do right by you in turn by recommending you to all their friends, family, and acquaintances.

Let us now move on to Chapter 8, where I will talk about the various ways you can pitch to the different kinds of clients you have.

CHAPTER 8
PITCHING

Every sale done in the history of mankind was based on an emotional experience.

In this chapter, you will learn how to effectively and efficiently solve a variety of problems regularly experienced in real estate. Basically, every purchase is based on a different scenario and every buyer has a different set of circumstances. A successful agent will be able to accommodate and work with each of them; remember, the client wants to move the money and it's your job to help them do so. That's why you need to be clever about how you do business! Let me give you some examples.

TAXES AND ELECTRONIC CURRENCY

Dubai is a very vibrant city that attracts people from all over the world. Europeans are very interested in buying in Dubai—it's sunny all year long and it's safe. Dubai is also a safe haven for investment; investors don't have to pay taxes on the properties they purchase, and they don't have to pay taxes on their capital gains from the property. And most importantly, they don't have to pay any taxes on the returns they get from the property. These are all tax-related issues in Europe that they simply don't have to face in Dubai. That's why they come here—and it's very important for us to be waiting for them with the proper knowledge and a very good payment plan. We have the added advantage of being able to give them very good financing options; any international investor can pay for 50% of the property, then be financed by the UAE banks for the remaining 50% for up to 25 years.

Other issues around the world also motivate them to buy in Dubai. For example, people are eager to avoid inheritance tax. Dubai offers everyone investing in freehold properties the choice to register under Sharia (the Islamic court) or under the DIFC rules (the British court). Usually, when you invest in a foreign country, you have to follow their rules; the advantage of investing in Dubai is that you get to choose which rules best suit you or your family. For example, under Sharia, the wife gets a percentage and the kids get a percentage, and you don't lose any to tax. This system therefore allows buyers to select which system they'd like to follow according to their individual circumstances.

Another example I wanted to give involves a situation in Lebanon, where most people's money is stuck in the banks, preventing them from doing anything with it. Now, we offer them the opportunity to invest in property in the UAE but pay for it in Lebanon, giving them the freedom to enjoy their money without being restricted.

A lot of people have their money tied up in cryptocurrency, and we are seeing that this market is very volatile—it goes up and down. For people wanting to buy properties using their cryptocurrency, multiple entities in the UAE are now accepting the direct transfer of Bitcoin, and some of them are signing up as multiple companies where they will liquidate the cryptocurrency and send it to the developer.

These are the types of solutions you need to be aware of. You are here to be the problem solver and to offer buyers all the proper knowledge, to detail all the factors involved and how they go about approaching and entering the market; you are here to help them alleviate the headaches and handle every obstacle that comes their way.

MORTGAGES

In order for you to be really specialised and get the most for these people, you need to understand bank mortgages and how they work. There are multiple types, including single mortgages, joint mortgages, and business loans. You need to be able to pitch these loans; this involves explaining how they work, as well as how many years they have to pay them off and what the interest rate will look like. Another key part when it comes to mortgages is releasing equity. Once the property is fully paid for, you can release 60% of the equity, meaning that the bank will give you this money in the form of cash and put the property back on a mortgage. For your first property, you can release equity of up to 60%. For the second, you can release up to 55%. For the third one, you can release up to 50%. This is a fantastic opportunity for someone to leverage their money by taking out the equity and investing it in more properties or more businesses, generating further income.

FINDING SOLUTIONS

Recently, I had a case where a family man, Lee, was living abroad; he saved his money, then went back home for visits. His family would put the money in the bank to earn interest. One day, he went back and all of the money was gone. His family eventually reached a point where they couldn't even afford food. Luckily, they contacted me to find out what they should do. On my advice, they had bought in Dubai. I resold this property and gave them the cash. And this family, they were so thrilled. It gave me such a beautiful feeling of satisfaction and happiness; the wife and the grandmother—*everyone*—they were all telling me, "God bless you; you changed our lives." I felt super noble. And that's something amazing. This is just one of the problems I have solved.

Another problem involved an investor who also had lots of investments back home, but the government was getting a share of almost 60% of it. After talking to this investor, I created a portfolio for him in Dubai, where he started generating money and getting all of the net income to himself. And he could not be happier. On a weekly basis, he calls me to thank me for this move. I've also helped lots of people get business loans. Previously, they had issues surviving markets, but after getting these loans, they've opened multiple branches, and now they're becoming very big organisations.

In summary, the more knowledge you have, the better the odds are for you to get a deal done. You solve these problems, and whatever is left is really easy and you can just go in and do it. Always give your best to get the results you want. The more you educate yourself about finance, the more solutions you will have for every problem—and trust me, for every problem, there is a solution.

I'll return to my earlier point regarding meeting people and making connections to develop a database of contacts. Establish great relationships with banks, with private lenders, and with every financial entity, because these people will always give you a solution for the situation your client or your potential clients might be facing. That way, if you don't know how to solve a problem, you can at least get in touch with someone who will.

Now it's time for the next chapter, which talks about following the cheese—running after the money, wherever it is.

CHAPTER 9

FOLLOW THE CHEESE

Money doesn't disappear, it goes into a cycle.

In this chapter, you will learn how to find and locate the money—how to approach it, how to target it, and how to become a money magnet. When it comes to money, the most important part is your objective: how much money you should be making per day and how much money you should be making per hour for you to reach your target. You'll find a spot at the end of this chapter for you to record your targets; it's a good idea to keep this somewhere you can see it on a daily basis to keep you on track towards achieving your money goals.

CONDUCT YOUR RESEARCH

In the sales business, we always see people putting in lots of effort. But unfortunately, this effort is often being put in the wrong places—where it's not productive, and it's not giving them any results. Instead, it's just backfiring on the sales representative; it's making him depressed, resentful towards his job, unproductive, feeling like everything is wrong around him. The only reason this is happening is that this person hasn't done his due diligence. It's very important to find out if you should be putting your effort into this part of the world or not.

For example, let's say that you're looking for fresh water—you're not going to drive to the desert to look for freshwater because that's not where the water is. Instead, go for a river or for a nice lake—that's where you'll be getting the water. And the same goes for our industry: the money is found in major corporations. The money is in the stock market, the banking and financial institutions, the hedge funds, the clubhouses, the luxury malls, and the outlets—and that's where you need to be. First, you need to do your prospecting. And that's why I say that prospecting is one of the most important aspects of our job.

FOLLOW THE CHEESE: BUSINESS PROFESSIONALS

Lots of investors like dividing their money. Some of them put 30% of their assets into real estate, 30% into gold, and the remaining 40% into the stock market. So when you approach the stock market, you will be approaching a successful stockbroker making 100,000 or even 1 million a month; you will meet with them to create an amazing relationship because it's going to be a mutually beneficial business. Any person making money from the stock market will want to transform it into a safe asset, and there is nothing safer than real estate. Say a different client wants to expand beyond real estate. You can refer this person to the stockbroker; similarly, the stockbroker can refer his clients to you if they want to enter the real estate market. In this way, there will be a cycle of money where everyone is taking a bite of the cake.

It goes the same way for the banking and financial institutions, as they are the ones that have the most investors. Most people don't have businesses—they're looking for mortgages or a home, they're looking for business loans. That's where you will find the money. It's the same at the hedge funds. A hedge fund is a group of investors who put all of their assets together and create some form of liquidity to invest, and the profits will be divided equally between the members. Whether it's a property, a business loan, or a hedge fund, there will be a manager or consultant who is overseeing it. They will have all the details of people who are looking to invest their money, so it is worth getting to know them so you can establish a business relationship and exchange information.

FOLLOW THE CHEESE: IN THE FIELD

A lot of rich people like to spend their time in clubhouses. Some of them have a poetry group and some are members of horse clubs, while a few others just like to have business groups. No matter what the club's interests are, there is always money there, and there are always people who know people who want to invest in property. If you become friendly with these clubs and their members, it will enable you to network and expand your client base. You know for a fact that these people have money, and in all likelihood, they want to spend it—that's where you come in.

The same goes for luxury malls. You know the scenario: they go out for a few hours of shopping and end up spending 20 or even 40 thousand dollars. Anyone who can spend that much in one shopping session has money to spend. Be smart. Approach the sales assistants, the store managers—get to know them. Chances are they've gained some insight into their customers when helping them out with their shopping, so they have a pretty good idea of who's who and who wants to buy what. It's just like the security guard scenario; if a customer tells the store manager at Chanel that they're looking at purchasing some real estate, you want the manager to drop your name. And again, it goes two ways—you'll be able to return the favour later on.

Again, don't be fooled into thinking that you can try one thing only and become successful. It's all about trial and error and covering all your bases. Liaise with multiple stockbrokers, with multiple financial institutions, with multiple luxury store managers. You don't have to work hard; you just need to work smart.

Take a pen and paper and note down who you know who might fall into the above-mentioned categories and try to figure out a way to approach them. Socialise, prospect. Don't be afraid to shake hands. Remember, the more shares, the more hands you shake, the more money you will make. And this leads us to the next chapter, which is about customer service.

MONEY TARGETS

HOURLY TARGET	DAILY TARGET	WEEKLY TARGET
Achieved? Yes / No	**Achieved? Yes / No**	**Achieved? Yes / No**

CHAPTER 10
CUSTOMER SERVICE

The happier they are, the more they're going to spread the word.

In this chapter, you will learn how to handle objections. You will learn how to be very attentive and always available, and how to deal with mistakes and come back with solutions. In customer service, you will be remembered for one of two things: your terrible service or your amazing service. No one will ever remember average service. So it's very important to give the experience of a lifetime. Imagine that you are the client. Now think about how you want to be approached, how you want to be contacted, how you want all your problems to be handled, and how you want to remember this person who was dealing with you.

THE BASICS

First, you need to make sure that your personal hygiene has been taken care of; you should be very well-dressed, always ready, and attentive. You're a professional, and you should look the part, down to the very last detail. Be friendly and polite—always. You must put a smile on your face, no matter what. Even if this person gets offended or loses their temper, you need to remember that it's not you. The person has come to you because they have a problem, and although there is a problem, there is also a solution. It's true, you might have nothing to do with their issues and problems, and you might wonder why they're taking it out on you. But you're the problem solver and your emotions shouldn't be involved in this at all. Rather, you should just use your brain, absorb the information, and take it. Once you've done this, you can then move on to the most important part of your customer service experience: problem solving.

FINDING A SOLUTION

For every problem, there is a solution, as has been true since the beginning of the history of humankind. And what makes us different as individuals is that some people will get offended, they will come back shouting, while some people will just listen, smile, offer a solution, guide the client, and give him the best experience of his life.

In our industry, we have lots of international clients, and these clients are not physically present. Remember, these people are trusting you with millions of dollars over the phone or over a Zoom call. So once you begin showing your knowledge, once you show them your credibility, you are giving the client a warm feeling—you are giving them a feeling like, *This person is interested in helping me manage my money. This person will manage my property or even my portfolio, and this person is gonna make me more money.* This will make the client feel like you are a real friend. It's not very hard to gain their trust, so long as you are extremely transparent, easy-going, and give them the right information. Don't try to fool anyone. Don't tell them something that is not true. Because at the end of the day, social media is everywhere, and anyone can verify information with the click of a finger.

When international investors want to know the location of Dubai, we can go to Google Earth and show them the exact location; we can also explain the previous transactions in that area, the rental market, the rental demand, why this area is an upcoming area or why it has so much demand, and where people should park their money. Sometimes, the investor's home country will not let them transfer big amounts of money. Your job is to find a solution—for example, sending invoices from developers with proof of documentation, such as a letter of intent saying that Mr X is buying a property from this development, that this is the actual contract sales purchase agreement, this is the reservation form, this is the amount that needs to be transferred, this is our escrow account, and so on. In this way, you will be helping him get his money out of the country without all the hassle.

Other people might have their money tied up in a cryptocurrency and they want to send it to Dubai. For some reason, developers don't accept Bitcoin transfers, so the money will need to be liquidated through a third party. Such third parties are readily available in this city, but you need to make connections with them first so that you can deliver the right information to your client. If you are able to guide them through the process and deliver accurate information, you will secure their trust and their respect. Rehearse different scenarios by putting yourself in the shoes of the client and visualising a solution that will make them happy. Anticipate problems and devise solutions; this will mean that you're ready for anything.

Always Follow Up

Some agents think that once the paperwork is signed and the money has been transferred, that's the end of their job. They're wrong. What will make you indispensable to clients is the follow-up. Don't just secure the sale then abandon them; check in to see how they are doing, ask if you can help them with anything else, provide recommendations on other services they can access, such as property managers or legal consultants. This is likely to be mutually beneficial; you help them out from start to finish and then throughout their ownership of the investment property, and they help you out with glowing recommendations and more business when they're looking to further invest their money in the future. This attention to detail and willingness to help them out will set you apart from the rest and make sure that they remember you, and for all the right reasons!

Once you see that the client is smiling, that means the job has been done perfectly. Once you hear him thanking you from the bottom of his heart, that means you're his friend, and you've just created yourself a beautiful business network.

REFLECTION: CUSTOMER SERVICE

In order to deliver great customer service, you have to think about the kind of service you'd like to receive. Use the space below to come up with a strategy that will set you apart from everyone else.

A TIME WHEN I EXPERIENCED TERRIBLE SERVICE ...	A TIME WHEN I EXPERIENCED FANTASTIC SERVICE ...

THREE WAYS I'M GOING TO OFFER STAND-OUT SERVICE:

CHAPTER 11
COURAGE

Now you have the tools for success, it's time to put in the hard and smart work.

Like many other people who have experienced success, I believe it is important to give back. In writing this book, I am hoping to help other people to realise their dreams and see them become a reality, because there is more pleasure in giving back than getting. This book is your tool; you have all the techniques that you need to get where you want to be. Now it is all down to you—how hungry you are and how badly you want it.

Remember, it is all about having courage. If, at the end of the day, you have a hundred dollars, you are a hundred times courageous; if you have a thousand dollars, you are a thousand times courageous. So have the courage to pick up the phone and make that call, to press record and start making videos, to chase the cheese. This book is your head start; I tried out 10,000 different ways to find what works and what doesn't. In order for you to become a successful person, you have to become a different person. I dropped the extravagant lifestyle and all the partying, and I traded it for the trinity of success. I began reading books and articles, setting goals, speaking with successful people; I began thinking about the future to become the best version of myself. I fed my mind, body, and soul.

When I first started, I just wanted to make enough money to make it through the day; I was in survival mode, and big goals were far from my mind. But once I made enough money to get by, I realised that I was thinking small. I decided to set the bar higher and make a little extra on top of that. Eventually, I made my first hundred thousand, and then my first million. But I didn't stop there. Instead, I realised that I could accomplish more and then more again. Each time I reached my goal, I set a new one, until eventually, I made over $530 million worth of sales in three years. I worked hard and I worked smart. So here's your final activity: decide on your first step and take that leap.

CONCLUSION

After six years of consistent work, I made it big in Dubai and saw my dreams come true. In this book, I have broken down all my best tips and tricks; it contains everything I learnt as a real estate agent in a city that is filled with opportunities. I hope you have enjoyed reading it.

Once you put it down, I want you to sit by yourself, think about how you want to make it big, and try to incorporate some of the techniques I have mentioned into your own life; I want you to change your mindset and strive to become the best version of yourself.

Should you have any questions about what I have mentioned here, or even about real estate, you can contact me through the contact details mentioned on the author bio page. I look forward to hearing from you. Until then, dream big and work towards it.

Further Information

Please don't hesitate to reach out to me if you have any further questions or would like to share your own success stories. If you want to learn more, follow me on social media. Here, you will find hundreds of ideas on how to promote yourself and build a client base using the many platforms available to you. If you're interested in learning more about the real estate industry in Dubai, my online academy has over fifty pre-recorded videos providing advanced knowledge on the rules and regulations of Dubai's real estate market. These will provide you with more insight into the methods and techniques that will help you reach your goals, from the day you get the job to when you're trying to build your own listings. I also offer one-on-one and group coaching; see my website for more details.

SOCIAL MEDIA:

LinkedIn: https://lnkd.in/fCKcdaP
Facebook: https://www.facebook.com/anthony.a.jaoude.9
Facebook fan page: https://www.facebook.com/Dubai Finestwealthmanager/

ONLINE ACADEMY:

To sign up for my online academy and develop advanced skills, see my website: https://anthonyjosephaj.com/course.

OTHER ONLINE SOURCES:

For useful examples of video content to engage with potential clients, head to my YouTube channel: https://lnkd.in/fCKcdaP.

If you're interested in hearing more about my rise to success in the real estate industry, check out this podcast: https://podcasts.apple.com/ae/podcast/dubai-stars-rise-to-the-top/id1525177766.

Lastly, for more information about Dubai's booming real estate market, check out https://instagram.com/anthony_aj_wit?igshid=10ja1dl2bxq3x.

AUTHOR BIO

Anthony Joseph, a serial and self-made entrepreneur, is the Associate Director of Provident Estate (the largest and most innovative real estate brokerage in Dubai) and the CEO of Primestay (a holiday homes company in Dubai, UAE).

In 2014, Anthony moved from his home country of Lebanon to Dubai, UAE with only a few hundred dollars in his hand. In just a few years, he achieved hundreds of millions of dollars in real estate sales and started a company of his own.

Anthony works with high-net-worth investors and end-user clients to understand their requirements and deliver the best solution within Dubai's dynamic and evolving property market. He even became the Top Producer at Provident Real Estate, breaking new records and helping the agency become award-winning real estate brokers of choice and win the top sales category in the Emaar awards 2020.

In addition to his incredible contribution to the real estate industry, Anthony has been continuously giving back to the community through mentorship and coaching programs, helping other aspiring entrepreneurs to achieve their goals.

He is also the host of the podcast *Dubai Stars*, where he interviews the real hustlers of Dubai, who came to the city with literally nothing and grew to become the top players of their game.

You can reach Anthony at: https://anthonyjosephaj.com/

LinkedIn: https://lnkd.in/fCKcdaP

Facebook: https://www.facebook.com/anthony.a.jaoude.9

Facebook fan page: https://www.facebook.com/DubaiFinestwealthmanager/

Instagram: https://www.instagram.com/anthony_aj_wit/

You can listen to his podcast at: https://podcasts.apple.com/ae/podcast/dubai-stars-rise-to-the-top/id1525177766

www.ingramcontent.com/pod-product-compliance
Ingram Content Group UK Ltd.
Pitfield, Milton Keynes, MK11 3LW, UK
UKHW040913300726
14061UKWH00007B/3

WANT ME TO HOLD YOUR HAND?

Are you interested in getting one-to-one help to secure your future through any of the below?

- Property evaluation
- Buying, selling, and leasing
- Property management
- Interior design/fittings
- Holiday home rental
- Furnishing and relocating
- Mortgages, business loans, and personal loans
- Cryptocurrency liquidation

Get in touch with me on Anthony@providentestate.com and I will be happy to help